KARATE KATA

AND APPLICATIONS

1

VINCE MORRIS & AIDAN TRIMBLE

STANLEY PAUL

LONDON·SYDNEY·AUCKLAND·JOHANNESBURG

Aidan: To my wife, Linda

Vince: To Toni

Stanley Paul & Co. Ltd
An imprint of Random Century Ltd
20 Vauxhall Bridge Road, London SW1V 2SA

Random Century Australia (Pty) Ltd
20 Alfred Street, Milsons Point, Sydney 2061

Random Century New Zealand Limited
PO Box 40-086, Glenfield, Auckland 10

Century Hutchinson South Africa (Pty) Ltd
PO Box 337, Bergvlei 2012, South Africa

First published 1990

© Vince Morris and Aidan Trimble, 1990

Set in 12pt Palatino (Linotron)
Printed and bound in Great Britain by
Scotprint Ltd, Musselburgh, Scotland

British Library Cataloguing in Publication Data

Morris, P. M. C. (P. M. Vincent)
  Karate Katas.
  1. Karate
  I. Title II. Trimble, Aidan
  796.8'153

ISBN 0 09 174099 1

Contents

Acknowledgements

The authors wish to thank the following people for their kindness and helpfulness:

In particular our good friend Keiji Tomiyama, Chief Instructor to Great Britain and Europe for Tani-ha Shito-ryu, for the calligraphy.

Harry Cook for assistance in obtaining the historical photographs.

Chris Hallam and Dave Hook for their help during the photo sequences.

The Sherwood Business and Conference Centre for coffee and room to spread out.

Dominique Shead for calm patience and understanding, plus lunches!

Roddy Bloomfield (well known expert in the art of Real Tennis and erstwhile stunt man) for his enthusiasm for this project.

Kata

Kata are a predetermined series of blocking, evading and countering techniques against single or multiple attackers, who may be armed or unarmed.

In a sense Kata are not peculiar to Eastern fighting arts. That is to say that the concept of providing an instructional manual is not, for these are to be found in many European languages covering arts ranging from medieval swordsmanship to modern-day boxing.

One element stands out, however, as being significantly different in the Oriental Kata. In the majority of cases the Kata are taught to students by example, only rarely were the early techniques recorded in diagrammatic or textual form, on scrolls which were kept secret and passed on only to exceptional students who had proved themselves worthy after many years practice.

Generally these secret scrolls contained brief details of the main instruction which was passed on orally and by example. They were often presented in a deliberately obscure fashion so as to be of little use if they fell into the hands of someone not well versed in the traditions and teachings of that particular school.

Gichin Funakoshi, the 'Father' of modern karate gives a revealing insight into the emphasis placed upon this secrecy.

In his book *Karate-do Nyumon* published in Japan in 1943 (and owing much to his third son Gigo [Yoshitaka] who is to a great extent responsible for the powerful Shotokan karate of today), Funakoshi relates that in the Ryukyu islands the tradition of secrecy was such that no written records were kept. Techniques were passed on by direct instruction from master to student, very often on a one-to-one basis, and the historical background to the Kata was transmitted by oral tradition, a notoriously imprecise method.

He goes on to tell of a communication he received from an elderly Okinawan karate-ka who wished to pass on to him a particular Kata before he died. As Funakoshi himself could not go, he asked that this Kata be taught to Gigo. After instructing Gigo in the

Kata (behind locked doors in a shuttered room) the old man confessed that he had refused to pass on this Kata to anyone before; only once in a crucially altered way to a man who had continually pestered him until he agreed.

Although in most cases the major concern of the scrolls is to catalogue the techniques of the Ryu, a good proportion of the text is given over to the element which distinguishes them from any Western instructional manual; the interweaving of spiritual philosophy with physical violence!

Based on an eclectic Zen Bhuddist foundation, with intertwining elements of Confucianism and the native Shinto religion, the art of despatching an enemy was raised to a spiritual level.

Indeed, so important was this Zen aspect that the same sentiments appear in scrolls of different Ryu, even in those concerned with distinctly different martial arts, such as Archery and Swordsmanship.

To come to a proper understanding of Kata, and to approach a proper practice of Kata it is vital to appreciate how inextricably interwoven is the philosophical element with the purely pragmatic physical side.

Just as this is so in the Kata of the older classical Ryu, so it is in the relatively younger 'schools' of karate, which have been subsumed into the traditional ethos.

Karate can indeed be practised purely as a strong and effective means of fighting. The Okinawan masters developed techniques capable of inflicting severe damage to any attacker and it is quite possible to train solely in the *waza* – the technique of blocking and counterattacking. Even the early practitioners of the art, however, held the spiritual element to be of equal importance to the physical techniques.

The Okinawan fighting arts were not themselves very much under the influence of the mainland Zen ethos, but *Te*, as the indigenous fighting art was known, became naturally subsumed into the martial culture and its Zen ethic upon its importation into Japan.

Even so, before this time there is evidence that certain Okinawan masters (Higaonna and Itosu, to name two) were much concerned that the art of *Te* be taught as a spiritually-orientated discipline.

After studying the history of karate, and indeed of all of the Japanese fighting arts, one has to conclude that it is a mistake to assume that they are inextricably involved with Buddhism, and with Zen in particular. What becomes clear, however, is that any discipline which removes the fear of death and injury, and enables trained reflexes to deal spontaneously and effectively with any threat is much sought after by the warrior.

The experience of the mainland warrior led to the development of a Zen-permeated martial culture, which, as well as imparting through strict discipline and meditation those very sought after qualities, also encouraged the development of individual values which were morally and socially beneficial: a concern for aesthetics and art, poetry and ceremony, belief in the virtues of honesty, dignity and compassion.

Toward the end of the sixteenth century, for example, the Jigen-ryu martial school, which was essentially concerned with teaching swordsmanship, established a curriculum which as well as concentrating on techniques with sword and dagger also devoted time to practice with spear and bow, and the art of poetry, and the tea ceremony. This was largely due to the influence of the Zen master Zenkicki.

Whether or not many actually attained those qualities which were held to epitomise the 'enlightened' man does not in any way detract from their desirability. The point to reflect upon is that in the original -*jutsu* form or in the later -*do* form a true martial artist is one who has attained mastery of both physical and spiritual aspects.

I have written in greater detail elsewhere *(The Karate-do Manual and The Advanced Karate Manual)* of the reasons why this emphasis on the spiritual side came about, but it is of such vital importance to correct understanding and application of Kata that the serious student must be encouraged to learn more of this aspect, and also fully understand that the spirituality – the *Zen* aspect – had a basic pragmatic reason for its emphasis, it made the martial artist a better fighter!

The essence of Zen is a complete acceptance of the inevitability of change; nothing remains the same, the wheel is always turning, leading to the only certainty – at some time or another this human lifespan will come to an end. To place too much importance on this fragile butterfly life was deemed futile; far better to aim at honour and respect, which held society together, even if in pursuance of this it became necessary to give up life. Thus the fighting man defeated his greatest foe – Fear! And specifically the fear of death, which if unconquered could cause that miniscule hesitation in combat that could be fatal.

Hence the importance placed upon gaining 'a mind like water'

This photo includes well known karate masters Chojun Miyagi, Koyu Konishi and Gichin Funakoshi. Funakoshi, far right, is the founder of Shotokan karate

(*mizu-no-kokoro*) in whose mirror-like surface all actions were reflected and perceived without the ripple of fear to distort the image, allowing the correct response to be made free of all inhibition.

The strict discipline of a continual regime of meditation based upon an acceptance of the transitory nature of all things led the samurai to develop a fearless disregard for the perpetuation of life at all costs, and to foster a strong-willed determination to continue upon a chosen course of action without hesitation, doubt or deflection. Indeed the basis of a formidable fighter!

Anyone, therefore, who wishes to fully understand and gain full benefit from practising the Kata must be prepared to at least consider carefully that to practise them purely as physical fitness forms or simply as a series of physical techniques is to go against the experience, advice and teaching of some of the most fearless and renowned fighters who ever lived!

There are some fifty Kata practised by the various karate schools today, mostly stemming from the practise and experience of the old masters, and in the Shotokan style we practice some 26 which can be broadly categorised into two groups: those which suit the larger, stronger martial artist, and those which are more appropriate to a lighter, more mobile stature.

The former group, which stress physical strength, were sometimes formally referred to as *Shorei-ryu*, and the latter, which emphasise speed and agility as *Shorin-ryu*, and although the *Shorei-ryu* type are particularly effective for physically conditioning the body it would be wrong to imagine that this was their main function, or that they were practised without the correct mental and spiritual concentration *(Zanshin)*.

Likewise, although the two types seem to suit essentially different body types it is a mistake to choose to concentrate solely on the group which, on the surface, would appear most appropriate to your particular build; all the Kata develop a rhythm and co-ordination of movement, and the well-balanced fighter must develop the attributes of both types.

At advanced level it is necessary to select one or two Kata, for in-depth practice, to 'enter deeply' into the soul of the Kata, and at this stage then it would be appropriate to select from the type most suitable to your physical characteristics. Even so the full range of Kata should not be neglected.

The problem

Although the physical practice of the various Kata is in itself an excellent physical exercise, promoting suppleness, flexibility and improved muscle tone, we have seen that this is only part of the story, and that proper practice demands that the martial artist develop *Zanshin* an alert, concentrated awareness of the totality of the situation, with an untroubled 'unstopping' mind allowing complete freedom for appropriate and effective action.

How?

'While performing a Kata, the karate-ka should imagine himself to be surrounded by opponents and be prepared to execute defensive and offensive techniques in any direction.' So urges the late head of the Japan Karate Association, Masatoshi Nakayama, who was himself one of Gichin Funakoshi's students. *(Best Karate*, Kodansha International Ltd, 1981.)

This to a student under the direct instruction of a master in a one-to-one learning environment, I suggest, is easier to comply with than is the case with the vast majority of karate-ka practising today.

We have seen that much of what is now included within the Kata has been passed on by oral tradition, subject to misperception, misunderstanding and plain forgetfulness, as well as by the deliberate desire to keep the original meanings secret, known only to a trusted few. Even some techniques which, on the face of it, are self-evident, may not be quite what they seem in the Kata, they – like many of the blocks – may be presented in the reverse of the proper direction.

Also we know that many of the Kata practised today have been deliberately altered to make them more suitable for mass transmission, as well as to make them conform to the more athletic nature of present-day techniques and upon occasion to make the practice of them safer. For example, whilst performing the Kata *Chinte* Kanazawa Sensei broke his right hand by striking the back with *Ipponken* causing Master Nakayama to remind him that the Kata should be modified for training purposes. All of which makes the practice of the Kata in line with Nakayama's advice practically impossible, as, in our experience, the vast majority of students have and can only have a rudimentary understanding of the *Bunkai* – the applications of the techniques contained within the Kata.

Takayuki Kubota, Head of Gosoku-ryu Karate in America (The International Karate Association), and well known as an instructor to Law enforcement agencies writes: 'At the moment most people that practise Kata have no idea of its real meaning, or the benefit that it brings. They practise Kata and Kumite as though they were two different things whereas of course Kumite starts with Kata and Kata starts with Kumite.'*

This being so, it is impossible that the Kata be practised fully and completely, and that proper *Zanshin* be exercised.

Yet another problem must be faced. To be practised as was originally intended, that is as a powerful and *effective* means of self-defence, with value in today's society, then it should be obvious that even if all the original *bunkai* were known practice solely related to them would be anachronistic; having little relevance. Sadly, in the world of today attackers are more likely to wield a razor-knife, broken beer-glass or even a gun than a *bo* or *jo*. This latter problem becomes more apparent when one realises that even within the confines of the history of the development of karate techniques the Kata are anachronistic in that they ignore many of the techniques which are widely (and effectively) incorporated into the basic practice of modern karate. Such techniques as: *mawashi-*

*Interview with David Chambers in *Fighting Arts* No. 54.

geri (roundhouse kick), *ushiro-mawashi-geri* (back roundhouse kick), *kakato-geri* (heel or axe kick) and *ushiro-geri* (back kick) are only a few which do not appear in the Kata.

Indeed, this problem exercised the current head of Shotokan Karate International, Hirokazu Kanazawa, to the extent that he began to incorporate *jodan mawashi-geri* into the Kata *Empi*. This move did not find favour, however, and the Kata is currently practised as before, with no roundhouse kick.

It would seem appropriate at some stage for senior *Sensei* to pool ideas and formulate a new Kata, based on the historic principles, but incorporating modern karate techniques.

Famous karate master Motabu showing high block

The myth

There is one widespread myth that needs dispelling before we consider the final section of this chapter, the precepts which must be borne in mind when practising the Kata, and that is the racial myth that mastery of karate, and in particular the Kata, is only attainable by the Japanese, for only they can have a real understanding of the martial ethos permeating the art, and can therefore achieve the highest levels of skill.

Frankly this is arrant nonsense!

Let us turn the premise around and hypothesise a native English sport, with philosophical connotations and obscure rules and rituals, deeply rooted in English tradition. Could we then safely assume that no-one but a native-born Englishman would ever excel in the sport, and that no Englishman would ever be beaten by a foreign competitor. Even a cursory glance at the record of the England Cricket team over recent years will serve to underline the ridiculousness of this idea!

Of course there are cogent (financial) reasons for the perpetuation of the myth of Japanese superiority, and indeed there may well be some Japanese who actually believe in it. This does not mean that anyone else need accept it. Indeed, when karate was first introduced to the West, the Japanese were naturally superior, both in skill and understanding, but also in the physical flexibility – especially in the hips and legs – which came to them as a direct consequence of the nature of their society, and which enabled them to have a greater facility in the techniques.

Japanese supremacy has now been challenged, just like the supremacy of English cricketers. At first the Japanese fighters were thought unbeatable, but the records show that the British team has defeated the Japanese on each of the last four occasions when they have fought. The most obvious example is Aidan Trimble's success in Tokyo, the heartland of Japanese karate, when he took on and soundly defeated the best of the world's Shotokan Karate International fighters, including the cream of the Japanese, to become the first World Openweight Kumite Champion.

The point I am going at lengths to make is an important one. If you place any credence in this myth then you set limits to your own progress. There are no limits within the art of karate, only those inherent in each individual practitioner. Believe this and put aside all negative inhibiting ideas.

How to Practise the Kata

As mentioned before, the mental attitude to Kata should be the same as for Kumite. The opponent must actually exist for you, or the Kata will be relegated to the level of mere physical calisthenics. In correct practice it is vital to maintain a sense of urgency and reality, and at every step envisage yourself as actually under threat and attack by a number of assailants determined to do you serious harm.

In this atmosphere *Zanshin* can be developed, and no technique need be 'pulled' short of the target through fear of inflicting damage, as in practice with a partner, and, furthermore, no time can be grabbed for regaining one's breath with these opponents, as they know no rules of fair-play, nor any referee's intervention!

Pragmatically, however, Kata training is a progressive experience which can roughly be defined in three stages.

To begin with, the student has enough to do simply trying to remember the sequence of techniques and changes of direction whilst keeping time to the teacher's count without trying to visualise 'real' opponents.

This is quite in order, for at this stage the technical proficiency and mental awareness are secondary to establishing the pattern of the Kata. Even so, during this process whilst the motor skills and underlying rhythms of the blocking and countering movements are being assimilated, the body is being strengthened, and balance and co-ordination enhanced.

The second stage of development commences when the pattern of the Kata has become firmly established, almost second nature. Now the emphasis is upon specific aims. The student strives to refine his practice, polishing technique and beginning to keep in mind the target areas, the appropriate application of speed and strength, and correct breathing. At this stage, under the direction of an experienced *sensei,* the student is put under increasing physical and mental pressure and begins to become aware of just how important is the power of the mind in physical activity. He or she learns to drag something extra from the depths of the psyche, a strength and stubborness that perhaps has never before been revealed. The body becomes so exhausted from obeying the *sensei*'s command: 'Hai! Now once more!' that it becomes impossible to even keep the eyelids open! Every breath becomes a painful gasp and seemingly must be the last, but even as the body staggers and weakens the spirit shouts: 'I will not give in!' – And from this the lesson is learned that in the depths of your spirit you can never be defeated.

The third stage is properly the practice of 'Moving Zen'. The techniques are by now instinctive and the goal perfection. Practice becomes an intensely private thing, age no longer matters, youthfulness, strength and stamina, even a fully operative body are not prerequisites for this journey. Here the Kata is never for simple display but is a vehicle, a path of absolute determined awareness and concentrated attention.

By this final stage the karate-ka has developed the ability to fuse mind, body and spirit to profound depths. The outward display is secondary to the manifestation of inner power and calm determination. Now the 'stopped' mind is released; fear is defeated by acceptance, and all peripheral anxieties are seen in perspective and set aside as full attention is directed to 'here and now'.

In Karate-do the Kata begin by being concerned with the physical down-to-earths of balance, co-ordination, power, flexibility and so on, but progress to being far, far more.

Each time a Kata is practiced (as a whole or in part – by a karate-ka thoroughly familiar with it) it should be a new creation, fresh, dramatic and meaningful in just the same way that a musician recreates a piece that has long featured in his repertoire. It should never be a stale repetition, a bored and boring rendition.

On the contrary, just as the musician 'loses' himself in his music so the karate-ka re-interprets and re-creates the Kata, bringing it to life and imbuing it with his own personality, making each performance the first.

There are occasions, however, when it is beneficial to perform the Kata in different ways. Hirokazu Kanazawa – one of the foremost karate teachers in the world – advocates that every third time it should be performed without power, directing the attention to maintaining *Hara* (concentrating *Ki* below the navel) and at the same time concentrating on the correct tensing and relaxing of the muscles.

Many teachers also advocate the practice of Kata in the opposite direction to the normal, thus affording practice on both sides and more deeply ingraining the sequence into the memory.

Tokyo University Karate Club training, 1930

Aidan and I both strongly advocate that you vary the direction in the *Dojo* in which you regularly practise. This will help ensure that you concentrate wholly on the Kata and the imaginary opponents rather than using a familiar object in your area of vision to help orientate you. Similarly, after taking care to make sure of safety, you should from time to time practise the Kata with your eyes closed.

For the karate-ka interested in Kata competition these last suggestions will be helpful in overcoming the problem of performing in an unfamiliar environment.

In our book *The Advanced Karate Manual* I gave a comprehensive outline of utilising visualisation techniques as an aid to practice. I will simply point out here that this method can prove invaluable in refining the execution and performance of Kata, and is strongly recommended.

A point worth making to the Kata competitor is that the idea of competition is essentially alien to the fundamental concept of Kata, which we have seen to be not for public display but as an aid to the effective execution of Kumite and self-defense. Following this, as Kanazawa comments, the essence lies not in the beauty of movement but in its efficiency.

In many instances today we find that Kata competitors vie with each other to perform the 'flashiest' most acrobatic Kata, complete with side-kicks that go straight up! Thus underlining how far from a proper understanding of their art are both the competitor and the judges who are impressed by external agility rather than internal condition manifested in simple, effective and efficiently executed techniques performed with *Zanshin*.

As a matter of course the *Bunkai* – the application of the techniques – should form part of regular practice with a partner. To make Kata performance meaningful it is necessary to visualise the attackers and their techniques as they would be in reality, and this means constant practice with partners to enable correct judgment of distance and timing.

To begin with the defenses should be the traditional ones which were originally devised to meet each particular attack. Only when thoroughly conversant with these should the *Bunkai* be altered.

If the Kata are not to be relegated to the status of museum pieces, however, it is important that they be applicable to the different circumstances of the modern age, wherein it is most unlikely that an attacker would wield a six-foot *Bo,* but baseball bat, knife, club or gun. Every type of weapon demands a different response in terms of recognising the potential of the weapon and assessing the correct defense. It is a good idea, therefore, to incorporate various weapons into *Bunkai* practice and modify the responsive technique, distance and timing to suit. Of course, by the nature of the Kata, by the secrecy surrounding them, through misunderstanding and by purposeful deception, and by the changes wrought by a variety of masters, it is not always clear just what the original meaning of any particular move was. If this is the case, then we advise consulting the original from which the Shotokan Kata evolved. This will very often provide the clue and help clarify the original purpose. Failing this, it is better to invent your own application than simply to practise the technique as calisthenics. Bear in mind, however, that the application must be efficient and effective, and follow properly from the one preceding and lead without forcing into the one following.

The precepts

The following points should be borne in mind when practising Kata:

Courtesy: karate begins and ends with courtesy, and is signified with the bow *(rei)* at the start and finish. It is important that the state of *zanshin* is apparent in the demeanour from the moment that the karate-ka walks forward to begin the Kata. The stance: heels touching, toes apart, hands lightly touching the thighs *(musubi-dachi)* should be relaxed but alert, the gaze directed straight ahead. A sense of calm determination should be cultivated as the mind and spirit is prepared for the encounters to come *(yoi no kisin)*.

All Kata should begin and end on the same spot on the line of performance *(embusen)*. Proper mastery is not attained until the breathing is harmonised with the execution of technique and posture *(kokyu)*.

Performing any element of the Kata without understanding turns it into an exercise in calisthenics and devalues the practice. You should always bear in mind the application and defend or attack the correct target areas *(tyakugan)* accordingly.

An error that we see quite often is the application of too much force and *kime*. It is important to understand that the Kata contain many movements which do not demand this. Master Funakoshi himself points out: 'The use of strength in continuous, rapid motions does not mean that one is skilled' *(Karate-do Kyohan)*. You must move quickly or slowly as necessary, and only apply strength where appropriate.

Remember that *Yame* at the end of a Kata carries the implication of a continuing state of readiness, so do not 'switch off'. To the true martial artist there is no dividing line between their art and 'real-life'. The art becomes the shaping and refining tool for moulding life, and in turn becomes inextricably an expression of that life. There can be, then, no 'switching off' until life ends.

Pragmatically of course, a state of unawareness has often brought about the sudden end of life!

Key

It is impossible to learn kata only from a book. A good instructor is vital. Diagrams and text should serve as aids to memory. This being so, the direction of movement has been indicated by what should be self-explanatory symbols, which indicate general movement, not necessarily the focus of attention.

NB: All Kata begin and end with the bow of respect *(Rei).*

Heian Shodan

This is now the first proper Kata in the Shotokan syllabus, in which training is given in basic and essential techniques: the stances *Zenkutsu-dachi* and *Kokutsu-dachi*, the blocks *Gedan-barai*, *Age-uke* and *Shuto-uke*. The Kata contains 21 movements, and takes approximately 40 seconds to perform. It should not be rushed. Pay attention to the rhythm of the movements.

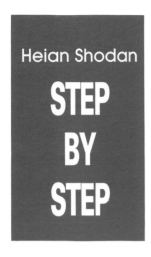

Heian Shodan

STEP
BY
STEP

1. Shizentai

2. Musubi-Dachi

3. Rei

8.

9. Zenkutsu-Dachi
Oi-Zuki

10.

11. Zenkutsu-Dachi
Gedan-Barai

16.

17. Zenkutsu-Dachi
Gedan-Barai

18.

19. Zenkutsu-Dachi
Age-Uke

4. *Yoi*

5.

6.

7. *Zenkutsu-Dachi Gedan-Barai*

12.

13. *Tetsu-Uchi*

14.

15. *Zenkutsu-Dachi Oi-Zuki*

20. *Zenkutsu-Dachi Age-Uke*

21. *Zenkutsu-Dachi Age-Uke. Kiai!*

KIAI

22.

23. *Zenkutsu-Dachi Gedan-Barai*

24. *Zenkutsu-Dachi Oi-Zuki*

25.

26. *Zenkutsu-Dachi Gedan-Barai*

27. *Zenkutsu-Dachi Oi-Zuki*

KIAI

32. *Zenkutsu-Dachi Oi-Zuki. Kiai!*

33.

34. *Kokutsu-Dachi Shuto-Uke*

35.

40. *Kokutsu-Dachi Shuto-Uke*

41. *Yame*

_ 28.

┼ **29.** *Zenkutsu-Dachi*
Gedan-Barai

┼ **30.** *Zenkutsu-Dachi*
Oi-Zuki

┼ **31.** *Zenkutsu-Dachi*
Oi-Zuki

36. *Kokutsu-Dachi*
Shuto-Uke

─┤ **37.**

─┤ **38.** *Kokutsu-Dachi*
Shuto-Uke

┼ **39.**

Heian Shodan APPLICATIONS

Figs 11-13 *Disengagement to hammerfist strike*

Figs 11-13 *(alternative bunkai) Forearm block to hammersmith strike*

Figs 18-19 *Openhand block, wrist grab, forearm strike to elbow*

Figs 38-40 *Knifehand block to knifehand strike*

d

Heian Shodan

SEQUENCES

Figs 1-10

Figs 11-22

Figs 23-34

Figs 35-41

Heian Nidan

This second training Kata gives further practice in the difficult backstance *Kokutsu-dachi*, rapid execution of consecutive techniques in one stance, simultaneous blocking and kicking whilst balanced on one leg etc., to a more complex rhythm than the first Kata.

It introduces many new techniques such as: *Mae-geri* and *Yoko-geri*, *Haiwan jodan-uke*, *Uraken-uchi* and *Shihon nukite*.

Containing 26 movements, this Kata should take approximately 50-60 seconds to perform.

Heian Nidan
STEP BY STEP

1. *Shizentai*

2. *Musubi-Dachi*

3. *Rei*

8. *Kokutsu-Dachi Chudan-Zuki*

9. *Kokutsu-Dachi*

10. *Kokutsu-Dachi Right Jodan Haiwan-Uke Left Ude-Soete*

11. *Kokutsu-Dachi Righ Nagashi-Uke Left Tetsui*

16. *Kokutsu-Dachi Shuto-Uke*

17. *Kokutsu-Dachi Shuto-Uke*

18. *Kokutsu-Dachi Shuto-Uke*

19.

KIAI

20. *Zenkutsu-Dachi Nihon-Nukite. Kiai!*

21.

4. *Yoi*

⊢ **5.**

⊢ **6.** *Kokutsu-Dachi Left Jodan Haiwan-Uke Right Ude-Soete*

⊢ **7.** *Kokutsu-Dachi Left Nagashi-Uke Right Tetsui-Uchi*

12. *Kokutsu-Dachi Chudan-Zuki*

⊢ **13.**

⊢ **14.** *Yoko-Geri-Keage Uraken*

⊢ **15.**

22. *Kokutsu-Dachi Shuto-Uke*

⟍ **23.** *Kokutsu-Dachi Shuto-Uke*

⊢ **24.** *Kokutsu-Dachi Shuto-Uke*

⟋ **25.** *Kokutsu-Dachi Shuto-Uke*

26. Zenkutsu-Dachi
Left Gedan Shuto-Uke

26a Front view of Fig. 26

27. Zenkutsu-Dachi

27a. Front view of Fig

30 Zenkutsu-Dachi

30a. Front view of Fig. 30

31. Zenkutsu-Dachi

32. Zenkutsu-Dachi
Left Uchi-Uke

38. Zenkutsu-Dachi
Gedan-Barai

39.

40. Zenkutsu-Dachi
Age-Uke

41.

28. *Zenkutsu-Dachi Right Uchi-Uke*

⊥ **28a.** *Front view of Fig. 28*

⊥ **29.** *Mae-Geri*

⊥ **29a.** *Front view of Fig. 29*

33. *Mae-Geri*

⊥ **34.** *Zenkutsu-Dachi Gyaku-Zuki*

⊥ **35.**

⊥ **36.** *Zenkutsu-Dachi Morote-Uke*

⊕ **37.**

42. *Zenkutsu-Dachi Gedan-Barai*

⊥ **43.**

KIAI

⊥ **44.** *Zenkutsu-Dachi Age-Uke. Kiai!*

⊥ **45.** *Yame*

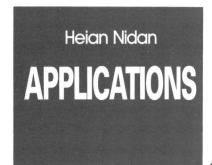

Heian Nidan
APPLICATIONS

Figs 6-8 a. Block

b. Deflection and strike to elbow

Figs 6-8 (alternative bunkai) a. Block

b. Arm lock

c. Back fist or hammer fist

Figs 13-16

b. Block and side snap kick to head

Fig 26 Straight fingers strike

Figs 26-29 Scooping block and mae-geri

Straight punch or hammer fist

a   b

Figs 19-20 *Pressing block and straight fingers strike*

Back elbow strike

e

e. *Alternative block and side kick to midsection (alternative bunkai to b)*

a   b

Figs 43-44 *Parry and rising forearm strike*

Heian Nidan

SEQUENCES

Figs 1-10

Figs 11-22

Figs 23-34

Figs 35-45

Heian Sandan

This Kata introduces one of the most difficult stances to master, *Kiba-dachi*, and continues training in multiple techniques from one stance. It gives practice in defending with the feet and elbows if the arms are restrained, and a response to an attack from the rear.

There are 20 movements in this Kata, which should take approximately 40 seconds to perform.

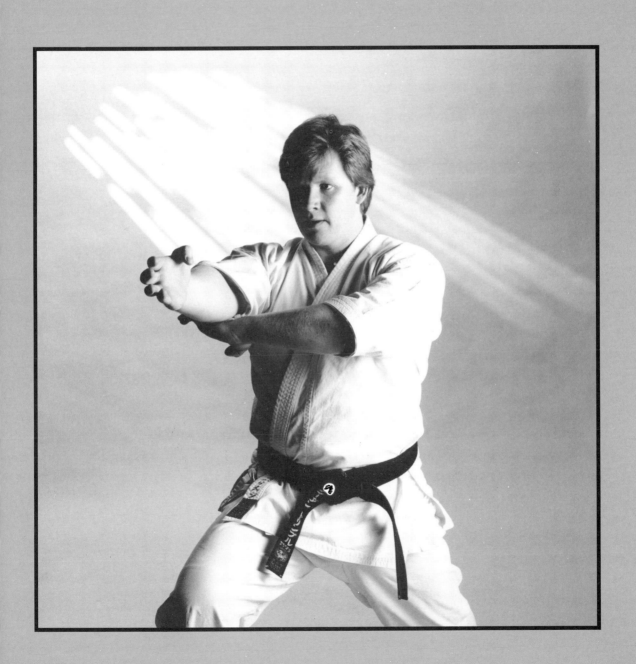

Heian Sandan

STEP BY STEP

1. *Shizentai*

2. *Musubi-Dachi*

3. *Rei*

8. *Heisoku-Dachi Kosa-Uke*

9.

10. *Kosa-Uke*

11.

16. *Heisoku-Dachi Kosa-Uke*

17.

18. *Kokutsu-Dachi Left Chudan Morote-Uke*

19. *Left Osae-Uke*

4. *Yoi*

5.

6. *Kokutsu-Dachi*
Left Uchi-Uke

7. *Heisoku-Dachi*

12. *Kokutsu-Dachi*
Right Uchi-Uke

13. *Heisoku-Dachi*

14. *Heisoku-Dachi*
Kosa-Uke

15.

20. *Zenkutsu-Dachi Right*
Chudan Shihon Nukite

21. *Turn*

22. *Turn*

23. *Kiba-Dachi*

24. *Kiba-Dachi Left Chudan Tetsui-Uchi*

25. *Step forward*

26. *Zenkutsu-Dachi Oi-Zuki. Kiai!*

KIAI

27. *Turn*

30a. *Front view of Fig. 30*

31.

31a. *Front view of Fig. 31*

32. *Kiba-Dachi Right Jodan Uraken-Uchi*

35. *Kiba-Dachi Left Empi-Uke*

36.

37. *Kiba-Dachi Left Jodan Uraken-Uchi*

38. *Kiba-Dachi*

28. Heisoku-Dachi
Ryoken Koshi Gamae

29. Mikazuki-Geri
Fumikomi

29a. Front view of Fig. 29

30. Kiba-Dachi
Right Empi-Uke

32a. Front view of Fig. 32

33. Kiba-Dachi

33a. Side view of Fig. 33

34.

39. Right Mikazuki-Geri
Fumikomi

40. Kiba-Dachi
Right Empi-Uke

41.

42. Kiba-Dachi
Right Jodan Uraken-Uchi

⊥ **43.**

⊥ **44.**

⊥ **44a.** *Front view of Fig. 44*

⊥ **45.**

⊥ **48.** *Step up*

⊕ **49.** *Turn*

⊥ **50.** *Kiba-Dachi Right Tate-Zuki Left Ushiro-Empi*

⊥ **51.** *Kiba-Dachi Right Tat Zuki Left Ushiro Empi. K*

45a. *Front view of Fig. 45*

46. *Kiba-Dachi Right Tate Shuto-Uke*

46a. *Front view of Fig. 46*

47. *Zenkutsu-Dachi Left Oi-Zuki*

52.

53. *Yame*

Heian Sandan
APPLICATIONS

Figs 6-8 *Block and disengagement from grab*

Figs 6-8 *(alternative bunkai) Disengagement from double lapel grab and counter with backfist to face and simultaneous*

Figs 20-24 *Spinning defence against grab or twisting arm-lock*

d

e

punch to stomach

e

Figs 20-24 *(alternative bunkai) Elbow strike to groin followed by shoulder wheel throw*

Figs 23-26 *Blocking attack – stamping kick counter. Blocking attack – back fist strike*

Figs 39-42 *Elbow and punch defence to grab from rear*

Figs 39-42 *(alternative bunkai) Lunge punch attack followed by shoulder throw*

SEQUENCES

Figs 1-10

Figs 11-22

Figs 23-34

Figs 35-46

Figs 47-53

Heian Yondan

Here the Kata more obviously begins to assume the characteristics of the traditional Kata from which it was drawn. It gives practice in the varieties of rhythm inherent in karate, the slow increase in tension on the one hand and the explosive release of powerful techniques on the other. Some of the more dangerous techniques of the traditional Kata are re-introduced, *Hiza-geri* to the opponent's face for example.

Comprising 27 movements, this Kata should take approximately 50 seconds to perform.

Heian Yondan

STEP
BY
STEP

1. *Shizentai*

2. *Musubi-Dachi*

3. *Rei*

8. *Kokutsu-Dachi*
Kaishu Haiwan-Uke

9. *Turn*

10. *Zenkutsu-Dachi*
Gedan Juji-Uke

11. *Step forward*

16. *Heisoku-Dachi*
Koshi-Gamae

17. *Yoko-Geri Keage*
Uraken-Uchi

18. *Zenkutsu-Dachi*
Left Empi-Uchi

19. *Zenkutsu-Dachi*
Left Shuto Gedan-Barai

4. *Yoi*

5. *Kokutsu-Dachi*

6. *Kokutsu-Dachi*
Kaishu Haiwan-Uke

7. *Kokutsu-Dachi*

12. *Kokutsu-Dachi*
Right Chudan Morote-Uke

13. *Heisoku-Dachi*
Koshi Gamae

14. *Yoko-Geri Keage*
Uraken-Uchi

15. *Zenkutsu-Dachi*
Right Empi-Uchi

20. *Zenkutsu-Dachi*
Right Jodan Shuto-Uchi

21. *Right Jodan Mae-Geri*

22. *Te-Osae-Uke*

KIAI

23. *Kosa-Dachi*
Right Uraken-Uchi. Kiai!

24. Turn
Kokutsu-Dachi

25. Kokutsu-Dachi

26. Kokutsu-Dachi
Chudan Kakiwake-Uke

27. Right Jodan Mae-Geri

32. Left Mae-Geri

33. Zenkutsu-Dachi
Left Oi-Zuki

34. Zenkutsu-Dachi
Right Gyaku-Zuki

35. Turn

39a Front view of Fig. .

KIAI

40. Right Hiza-Ate. Kiai!

40a Front view of Fig. 40

41. Turn

_ **28.** *Zenkutsu-Dachi*
  Chudan Oi-Zuki

↘ **29.** *Zenkutsu-Dachi*
  Left Gyaku-Zuki

✓ **30.** *Turn*

✓ **31.** *Kokutsu-Dachi*
  Chudan Kakiwake-Ure

_ **36.** *Kokutsu-Dachi*
  Left Chudan Morote-Uke

┼ **37.** *Kokutsu-Dachi*
  Right Chudan Morote-Uke

┼ **38.** *Kokutsu-Dachi*
  Left Chudan Morote-Uke

┼ **39.** *Zenkutsu-Dachi*
  Morote Kubi Osae

_ **42.** *Kokutsu-Dachi*
  Left Shuto-Uke

┼ **43.** *Kokutsu-Dachi*
  Right Shuto-Uke

┼ **44.** *Yame*

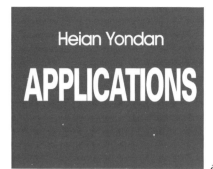

Heian Yondan
APPLICATIONS

Figs 5-6 Block to knife hand strike

Figs 10-12 Block kick and disengage from wrist grab and push

Figs 13-15 Simultaneous block and counter followed by elbow strike

Figs 19-23 a.b. Block kick and counter with knife-hand strike

c.d.e. Front kick,

Fig 6 *(alternative bunkai) Simultaneous block and backhand strike*

... down punching attack and counter with backfist strike

a   b   c

Figs 19-23 (alternative bunkai) Deflect kick, block punch and apply armlock follow front kick

a   b   c

Figs 24-29 Force apart opponent's arm and counter with front kick and two punches

a   b   c

Figs 38-42 From double block slide in and deflect punch, grab head and deliver knee smash. Follow by back elbow strike whilst turning to face next opponent.

Heian Yondan

SEQUENCES

Figs 1-10

Figs 11-22

Figs 23-34

Figs 35-44

Heian Godan

The final Kata in the training Kata series, as would be expected, gives practice in a variety of advanced techniques including successive upper and lower blocks *Gedan Juji-uke*, *Jodan Haishu Juji-uke*, and *Chudan Osae-uke*, plus distinct changes of height and rhythm. A bold-spirited Kata exemplifying the Shotokan spirit.

Containing 23 movements, the Kata should take about 45-50 seconds to perform.

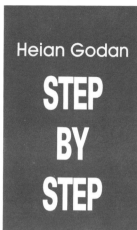

Heian Godan

STEP BY STEP

1.

2. *Heisoku-Dachi*

3. *Rei*

8. *Heisoku-Dachi*
Left Kagi Gamae

9. *Kokutsu-Dachi*
Right Uchi-Uke

10. *Kokutsu-Dachi*
Left Gyaku-Zuki

11.

16.

17. *Zenkutsu-Dachi*
Jodan Haishu-Juji-Uke

18.

19. *Zenkutsu-Dachi*
Chudan Osae-Uke

4. *Yoi*

5. *Kokutsu-Dachi*
Left Uchi-Uke

6. *Kokutsu-Dachi*
Right Gyaku-Zuki

7. *Turn*

12. *Heisoku-Dachi*
Right Kagi-Gamae

13. *Kokutsu-Dachi*
Right Chudan Morote-Uke

14. *Step forward*

15. *Zenkutsu-Dachi*
Gedan Juji-Uke

20. *Step forward*

21. *Zenkutsu-Dachi*
Oi-Zuki Chudan. Kiai!

22. *Mikazuki-Geri*
Fumikomi

23. *Kiba-Dachi*
Right Gedan-Barai

KIAI

╀ **24.** *Turn*

╀ **25.** *Kiba-Dachi*
   Chudan Haishu-Uke

╀ **26.** *Mikazuki Geri*

╀ **27.** *Step forward*

╀ **32.** *Turn*

⬦ **33.** *Jump. Kiai!*

╀ **34.** *Kosa-Dachi*
   Gedan Juji-Uke

╀ **35.** *Turn*

╀ **40.** *Kokutsu-Dachi*
   Manji-Gamae

╀ **41.** *Heisoku-Dachi*
   Manji-Gamae

╀ **42.** *Turn*

╀ **43.** *Heisoku-Dachi*
   Manji-Gamae

28. Kiba-Dachi
Right Empi-Uchi

29. Turn

30. Kosa-Dachi
Chudan Morote-Uke

31. Reinoji-Dachi
Koho-Zuki Age

36. Zenkutsu-Dachi
Right Morote-Uke

37. Turn

38. Zenkutsu-Dachi Left Nagashi-
Uke Right Gedan Shuto-Uchi

39.

44.

45. Zenkutsu-Dachi
Right Nagashi- Uke
Left Gedan Shuto-Uchi

46.

47. Yame

Heian Godan
APPLICATIONS

Figs 6-8 Block-counter punch. Grasp attacking arm and strike to elbow

Figs 6-8 (alternative bunkai) Grasp attacking arm and apply armlock

Figs 15-21 Block kick, block punch. Twist arm to unbalance opponent, palm-heel strike followed by lunge-punch

with forearm

Figs 29-31 *Block punch and strike to jaw*

Figs 30-32 *Block punch and simultaneously strike to jaw. Block second punch, grasp arm and throw*

Figs 37-41 a.b.c. *Deflect punch and strike to groin*

Figs 37-41 *(alternative bunkai) Block punch and counter with palm heel strike to groin. Block second punch and counter with hammer-*

Figs 37-41 *(alternative bunkai) Block kick, then block punch, simultaneously strike to groin, grasp, lift and throw*

d.e. *Grasp and throw attacker*

fist strike to ribs, simultaneously sweeping attacker's front leg

Heian Godan

SEQUENCES

Figs 1-10

Figs 11-22

Figs 23-34

Figs 35-46

Fig 47

Tekki Shodan

Ankoh (Yasutsune) Itosu, an Okinawan karate master, revised and adapted older Kata. Himself a student of the legendary Sokon Matsumura, Itosu was the great formulator and developer of Kata, and according to Funakoshi it was from Master Itosu that he learned the *Heian* and three *Tekki* Kata amongst others.

He specialised in the Tekki Kata and made Funakoshi spend three years learning each, admonishing that they were at once the easiest to learn but also the most difficult to learn.

The original name *Naihanchi* was changed to *Tekki* by Funakoshi, and although *Tekki Shodan* is an old *Shuri-te* Kata, *Nidan* and *Sandan* were created by Itosu as strengthening and training Kata, basing them upon the original but eliminating the dangerous techniques.

Originally performed in Naihanchi-dachi and Hachi-ji-dachi, they are now all performed in Kiba-dachi.

One of the most difficult techniques to perform correctly in *Tekki Shodan* is *Nami-gaeshi* the 'Returning wave' deflection. Many students incorrectly slap the instep against the inside of the thigh. The foot should travel to the front of the thigh to block or deflect a kicking attack.

The *Tekki* Kata should be practised assiduously in order to promote flexibility and lower body strength.

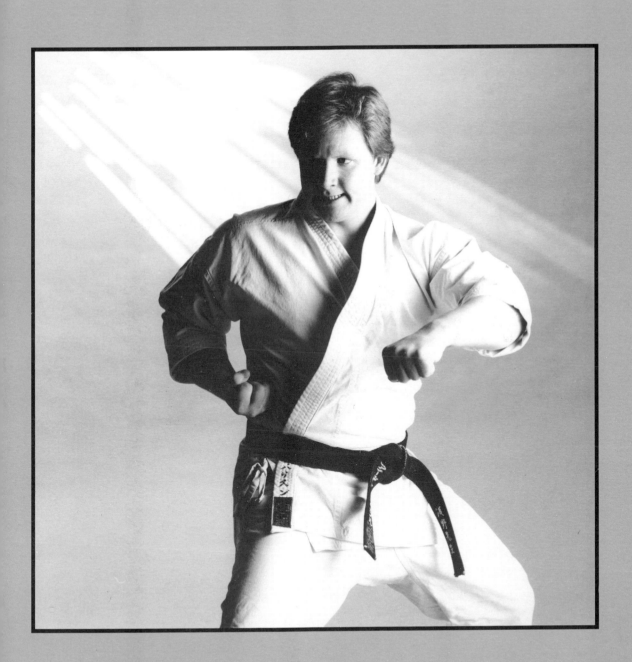

Tekki Shodan

STEP BY STEP

1. Shizentai

2. Musubi-Dachi

3. Rei

9. Kiba-Dachi
Koshi-Gamea

10. Kiba-Dachi
Gedan-Barai

11. Kiba-Dachi
Right Kagi-Zuki

12. Kosa-Dachi

17. Kiba-Dachi
Left Jodan Ura-Zuki

18.

19. Left Nami-Ashi
(Nami-Gaeshi)

20. Kiba-Dachi
Sokumen-Uke

Yoi + **5.** *Kosa-Dachi* + **6.** *Fumikomi* + **7.** *Kiba-Dachi Haishu-Uke* + **8.** *Kiba-Dachi Sokumen Empi*

13. *Fumikomi* + **14.** *Kiba-Dachi Right Uchi-Uke* + **15.** + **16.** *Kiba-Dachi Jodan Nagashi-Uke*

+ **22.** *Right Nami-Ashi (Nami-Gaeshi)* + **23.** *Kiba-Dachi Sokumen-Uke* + **24.** *Kiba-Dachi Koshi-Gamae*

KIAI

├─ **25.** *Kiba-Dachi*
Morote-Zuki. Kiai!

├─ **26.** *Kiba-Dachi*

├─ **27.** *Kiba-Dachi*
Haishu-Uke

├─ **28.** *Kiba-Dachi*
Sokumen-Empi

┤─ **33.** *Fumikomi*

┼─ **34.** *Kiba-Dachi*
Left Uchi-Uke

┼─ **35.**

├─ **36.** *Kiba-Dachi*
Right Jodan Nagashi-Uke

┤─ **41.**

├─ **42.** *Left Nami-Ashi*
(Nami-Gaeshi)

├─ **43.** *Kiba-Dachi*
Right Sokumen-Uke

├─ **44.** *Kiba-Dachi*
Koshi-Gamae

29. *Kiba-Dachi*
Koshi-Gamae

30. *Kiba-Dachi*
Right Gedan-Barai

31. *Kiba-Dachi*
Left Kagi-Zuki

32. *Kosa-Dachi*

37. *Kiba-Dachi*
Right Jodan Ura-Zuki

38.

39. *Right Nami-Ashi*
(Nami-Gaeshi)

40. *Kiba-Dachi*
Right Sokumen-Uke

45. *Kiba-Dachi*
Morote-Zuki. Kiai!

46.

47.

48. *Yame*

Tekki Shodan
APPLICATIONS

a   *b*

Figs 6-7 *Deflect punch attack grasp arm and attack with stamping kick to knee*

a   *b*   *c*

Figs 7-8 *Block punch, grab opponent, elbow strike*

a   *b*   *c*

Figs 32-35 *Block punch, simultaneously counter punch to stomach whilst blocking second punch. Strike to jaw with back fist*

28-29 *Block punch counter with hook punch*

Figs 36-37 a. *Block kick attack*   **b.** *Block punch attack*

36-37 *(alternative bunkai) Snap up to avoid sweep attack, slide in to follow-up spinning back kick*

Tekki Shodan

SEQUENCES

Figs 1-10

Figs 11-22

Figs 23-34

Figs 35-46

Figs 47 and 48

Bassai-Dai

A strong, powerful Kata, and one of the earliest, also called Passai. The techniques contained are not vastly more difficult than those already mastered in the *Heian* Kata, but implying the concept of strength and will strong enough to storm a fortress, this Kata exemplifies the idea of changing disadvantage – an initial attack – into advantage by strong and courageous response.

Although a Kata containing many vigorous elements, it is from the *Shorin-ryu,* and therefore the feeling of the Kata should be of precise, fast execution of technique, with due attention given to the appropriate balance between speed and power.

Containing 42 movements, the Kata should take just over a minute to perform.

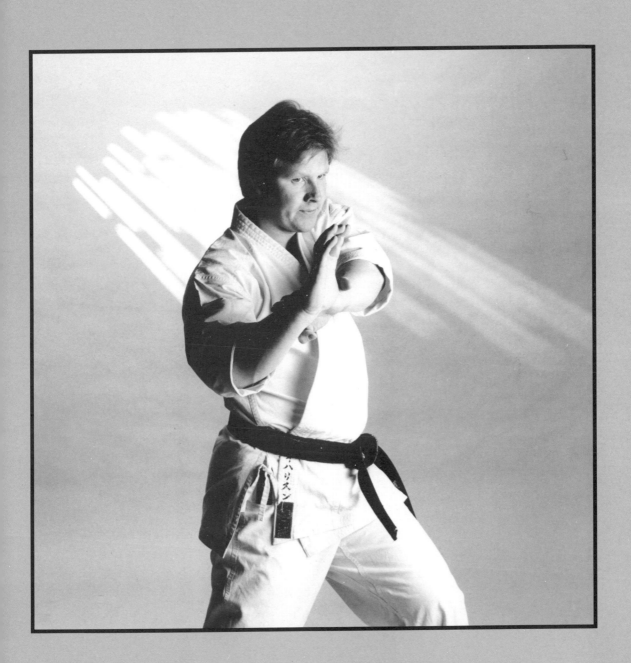

Bassai-Dai

STEP BY STEP

1. *Shizentai*

2. *Musubi-Dachi*

3. *Rei*

8. *Zenkutsu-Dachi Left Chudan·Uchi-Uke*

9.

10. *Zenkutsu-Dachi Gyaki-Hanmi Chudan Uchi-Uke*

11. *Turn*

16.

17. *Zenkutsu-Dachi Right Chudan Soto-Uke*

18.

19. *Zenkutsu-Dachi Gy Hanmi Chudan Uchi-U*

_ *4.* Heisoku-Dachi

┼ *5.*

┼ *6.* Kosa-Dachi
Right Uchi-Uke

╓ *7.* Turn

_ *12.* Zenkutsu-Dachi Gyaku-
Hanmi Chudan Soto-Uke

┼ *13.*

┼ *14.* Zenkutsu-Dachi
Right Chudan Uchi-Uke

┼ *15.* Gedan Sukui-Uke

_ *20.*

┼ *21.* Shizentai
Koshi-Gamae

┼ *22.* Shizentai Left
Chudan Tate Shuto-Uke

┼ *23.* Shizentai
Right Chudan-Zuki

┼ *24.*

25. Right Chudan Uchi-Uke

26. Shizentai
Left Chudan Zuki

27.

28. Left Chudan Uchi-Uk

33. Kokutsu-Dachi
Right Shuto-Uke

34. Kokutsu-Dachi (step-back) Left Shuto-Uke

35.

36. Right Tsukami-Uke
Left Soete

41. Heisoku-Dachi. Step back

41a. Front view of Fig. 41

42.

29.

30. *Step forward*

31. *Kokutsu-Dachi Right Shuto-Uke*

32. *Kokutsu-Dachi Left Shuto-Uke*

37.

38. *Gedan Fumikomi*

39. *Turn Kokutsu-Dachi Left Chudan Shuto-Uke*

40. *Kokutsu-Dachi Right Chudan Shuto-Uke*

42a. *Front view of Fig. 42*

43. *Heisoku-Dachi Morote-Age-Uke*

43a. *Front view of Fig. 43*

44.

44a. *Front view of Fig. 44*

45. *Zenkutsu-Dachi Chudan Tetsui-Hasami-Uchi*

45a. *Front view of Fig. 45*

46. *Zenkutsu-Dachi. S forward Right Chudan Oi-Z*

50. *Kiba-Dachi Left Chudan Haishu-Uke*

50a. *Side view of Fig. 50*

51. *Right Mikazuki-Geri*

52. *Kiba-Dachi Right Empi-Uchi*

54a. *Side view of Fig. 54*

55. *Kiba-Dachi. Right Gedan-Barai Left Soete*

55a. *Side view of Fig. 55*

56. *Turn. Zenkutsu-Dachi Koshi Gamae*

46a. *Front view of Fig. 46*

47. *Turn Mikazuki-Geri*

48. *Kiba-Dachi Right Gedan-Barai*

49. *Turn*

52a. *Side view of Fig. 52*

53. *Kiba-Dachi. Right Gedan-Barai Left Soete*

53a. *Side view of Fig. 53*

54. *Kiba-Dachi. Left Gedan Barai Right Soete*

56a. *Side view of Fig. 56*

57. *Zenkutsu-Dachi Yama Zuki*

57a. *Side view of Fig. 57*

58. *Heisoku-Dachi Koshi-Gamae*

58a. Side view of Fig. 58

59. Mikazuki-Geri

59a. Side view of Fig. 59

60. Zenkutsu-Dachi Yama-Zuki

62a. Side view of Fig. 62

63. Zenkutsu-Dachi Yama Zuki

63a. Side view of Fig. 63

64. Turn

69. Zenkutsu-Dachi Left Gedan Sukui-Uke

70. Half-step

71. Kokutsu-Dachi Chudan Shuto-Uke

72. Turn

60a. Side view of Fig. 60

61. Heisoku-Dachi Koshi-Gamae

61a. Side view of Fig. 61

62. Mikazuki-Geri

65.

66. Zenkutsu-Dachi Right Gedan Sukui-Uki

67.

68.

73. Half-step

74. Kokutsu-Dachi Chudan Shuto-Uke. Kiai!

75.

76. Yame

Bassai-Dai
APPLICATIONS

a

b

Figs 5-6 *As opponent attacks slide in and jam attack, simultaneously strike to jaw*

a

b

c

Figs 7-10 *Block punch, deflect and block second punch, grasp opponent and attack with front kick to stomach or groin*

a

b

c

Figs 15-19 *(alternative bunkai) With scooping block, hook away attacking leg, block punch and finish with kick to stomach*

Figs 15-16 Block kick with scooping block and counter with palm heel strike

a   b   c

Figs 22-29 Block punch with knife-hand block, punch to midsection, with the same arm deflect attacker's arm and punch

a   b   c

Figs 34-38 Block punch, block second punch. Grasp attacker's arm and counter with thrust kick to inside of knee

a   b   c

Figs 34-38 (alternative bunkai) Block punch, grasp and twist arm, counter with thrust kick to hip joint

a   b   c

e

again to midsection, snapping fist up to strike attacker's face

e

f

Figs 35-36 *Opponent grasps your wrists. Trap his hand on yours, in a clockwise circular motion cut into his wrist joint with your knife-hand*

a   *b*   *c*

Figs 42-46 *Block punch or disengage from double lapel grab. Attack double hammer-fist strike followed by lunge punch*

a   *b*   *c*

Figs 47-48 *Draw back blocking punch, spin and attack opponent's head with crescent kick and strike opponent's elbow with your forearm*

a   *b*

Figs 59-60 *Block kick with inside of shin and simultaneously counter-punch to jaw and groin*

a

Figs 50-55 *Block punch attack and counter with crescent kick, elbow strike to solar plexus and bottom-fist strike to groin. Block*

punch and strike again to groin

Figs 70-72 *Deflect punch, step in and strike to throat, sweep opponent to rear*

Bassai-Dai
SEQUENCES

Figs 1-10

Figs 11-22

Figs 23-34

Figs 35-46

Figs 47-58

Figs 59-70

Figs 71-77

APPENDIX

For those who would like to read further on some of the subjects dealt with in this book, we recommend the following magazines:

Magazines

American Karate, Ed. David Weiss, 351 West 54th Street, New York, NY 10019, USA.

Combat, Ed. Bey Logan, 135 Aldridge Road, Perry Barr, Birmingham B42 2ET.

Fighting Arts International, Ed. Terry O'Neill, PO Box 26, Birkenhead, Merseyside L43 4YQ.

Martial Arts Illustrated, Ed. Bob Sykes, Revenue Chambers, St Peters Street, Huddersfield HD1 1DL.

Shotokan Karate Magazine, Ed. John Cheetham, 1 Grove Court, Lymm, Cheshire.

Traditional Karate, Ed. Bey Logan, 135 Aldridge Road, Perry Barr, Birmingham B42 2ET.

Useful Addresses

The Federation of Shotokan Karate, PO Box 47, West PDO, Nottingham NG8 2EA.

The National Coaching Foundation, 4 College Close, Beckett Park, Leeds LS6 3QH.